EVOLUTION

ALVIN SILVERSTEIN • VIRGINIA SILVERSTEIN • LAURA SILVERSTEIN NUNN

TWENTY-FIRST CENTURY BOOKS

BROOKFIELD, CONNECTICUT

Cover photograph courtesy of The National Audubon Society Collection/Photo Researchers (© John Koivula).

Photographs courtesy of Visuals Unlimited: pp. 4 (© Cabisco), 8 (© Kjell B. Sandved), 17 (© Ken Lucas), 18 (© Kjell B. Sandved), 26 (© Walt Anderson), 27 (© Bruce Berg), 33 (© M. D. Maser), 37 (© Gurmankin/Morina), 40 (© Mack Henley), 43 (© Cabisco); The National Audubon Society Collection/Photo Researchers: pp. 7 (left © R. Dev, right © Catherine Ursillo), 21 (© Dan Levy), 29 (© Douglas Faulkner), 34 (© R. Noonan), 51 (© Jacques Jangoux); Corbis-Bettmann: pp. 10, 15; Photo Researchers: pp. 12 (© John Reader/SPL), 46 (© Francois Ducasse/Rapho), 50 (© Hank Morgan/Science Source)

Library of Congress Cataloging-in-Publication Data

Silverstein, Alvin.
Evolution / Alvin and Virginia Silverstein and Laura Silverstein Nunn.
p.   cm. — (Science concepts)
Includes bibliographical references (p.   ) and index.
Summary: Discusses early theories of evolution, the work of Darwin, fossil and other evidence, and the effects of evolution on us and the future.
ISBN 0-7613-3003-8 (lib. bdg.)
1. Evolution (Biology)—Juvenile literature. [1. Evolution.]
I. Silverstein, Virginia B. II. Nunn, Laura Silverstein. III. Title.
IV. Series: Silverstein, Alvin. Science concepts.
QH367.1.S55   1998
576.8—dc21   98-9278
                                                                                             CIP
                                                                                              AC

Published by Twenty-First Century Books
A Division of The Millbrook Press, Inc.
2 Old New Milford Road
Brookfield, Connecticut 06804

CONTENTS

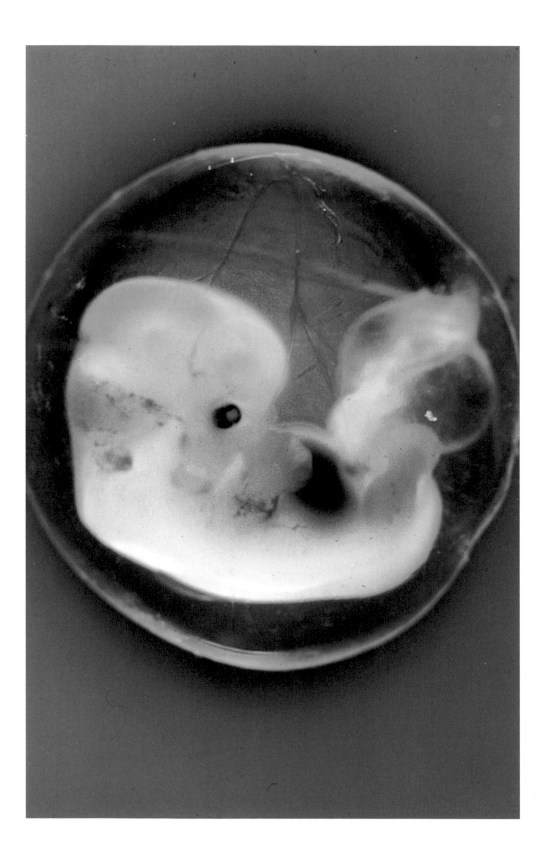

ONE

A Changing World

Life is full of changes. When a family moves into a new neighborhood, all of its members experience changes in their lives. Learning to adjust to a new school or a new job is not easy. Starting all over and making new friends are just as challenging. Some people have a more difficult time than others, but we all learn to adjust because it is necessary for survival.

People make changes and adjustments in their lives every day. They do it so they can function in society. The same is true for all living things, including plants and animals. For instance, when builders come into the wilderness and cut down trees to make room for a new development, some animals in the area may die as a result, but some will adapt to the new conditions and others will move on and adjust to a new environment. Pollution in the environment may be deadly to certain plants, but others are able to adjust to the change.

Many scientists believe that our world has been continually changing for billions of years through a process called **evolution**. The theory of evolution explains how the earth and all the living things on it have formed and developed, generation after generation. According to this theory, life first appeared about 3 to 4 billion years ago, after the earth's crust had formed and cooled. The first living things were very simple—just a collection of chemicals held together in microscopic blobs. As time passed, these simple organisms changed and developed—evolved—into more complex organisms that were better adapted to survive in their environment. Some became specialized in different ways, adapting not only to the conditions on earth but also to each other. Some of the new organisms could make their own food; others got energy and building materials by eating living organisms. They passed on their specialized characteristics to new generations, which evolved into an ever-greater variety of new forms. This process of evolution eventually produced all the species that live on the earth today.

✦ WHAT IS A SPECIES? ✦

The term *species* is Latin for "appearance" or "kind." Originally, **species** of organisms were identified by their appearance, since members of a species usually looked similar. In the eighteenth century, Swedish botanist and naturalist Carl Linnaeus classified plants and animals in different species depending on their physical characteristics. This method is still used to classify species, but it alone is not completely accurate. For instance, dogs exist in a variety of shapes and sizes, from the enormous Great Dane to the tiny Chihuahua, but all dogs belong to the same species. Some other kinds of living organisms may look similar to one another but do not belong to the same species. For example, the African elephant and the Indian elephant may look very similar, but they belong to two different species.

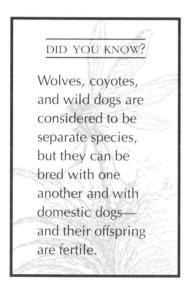

DID YOU KNOW?

Wolves, coyotes, and wild dogs are considered to be separate species, but they can be bred with one another and with domestic dogs— and their offspring are fertile.

Another key part of the species concept is that members of a species can breed with one another to produce fertile offspring. But members of one species do not usually breed with those of a different species. Dogs and cats do not belong to the same species. They cannot mate and produce little cogs and dats. African and Indian elephants, in spite of their similar appearance, cannot mate with each other.

The discovery of DNA, the chemicals that carry genetic information that is passed on from one generation to the next, has allowed modern scientists to define species more precisely. Genetic testing, for example, shows that all dogs, no matter what they look like, have DNA that is very similar. The DNA of African elephants, however, is quite different from that of Indian elephants, confirming that they do belong to different species.

A species can also be described as a particular group or population of living organisms that live in a particular area. Some species consist of only one population in a single area, such as an island. Other species include more than one population, each in a different location. For instance, gray squirrels can be found in a number of different areas, including North America, South Africa, and England. Unlike many other animals, gray squirrels are famous for adapting well to life in urban areas.

CROSSING SPECIES

When an organism of one species breeds with one from another species, their offspring are usually sterile. For instance, a male lion bred with a female tiger will produce a hybrid (offspring of two different species) known as a liger, which is unable to reproduce. Ligers exist only in captivity and have never been found in the wild. Other hybrids include zebronkeys—which are produced when a zebra breeds with a donkey—and mules, the result of a horse breeding with a donkey.

It is apparent from the size of the ears and the shape of the head that the Indian elephant (left) *and the African elephant* (right) *belong to different species.*

According to the theory of evolution, species have gradually changed, generation after generation. Many species that lived on the earth millions of years ago look very different from their descendants. But how do we know what species looked like millions or billions of years ago? **Fossils** (preserved skeletons or other remains) of plants and animals have been found all over the world. These fossils have provided a wealth of information for scientists.

Scientists are able to produce a fossil record by putting pieces of fossils together like a puzzle and by carefully analyzing the area where the fossils were found. Scientists can determine what the species looked like, what its classification was, and the time in history that it lived. Dinosaurs and saber-tooth tigers, which are now extinct (species that died out), are known only by their fossils. Paleontologists (scientists who study geological **periods** from fossil remains) believe that more than 99 percent of all the species that ever existed are now extinct.

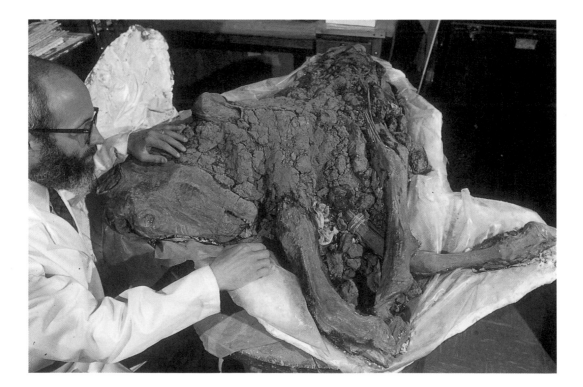

The earliest ancestor of the horse lived about 55 million years ago. By about 3 million years ago, the horse, like this Cenozoic Era fossil, looked somewhat like modern horses.

TWO

THEORIES OF EVOLUTION

"Everybody knows" that the English naturalist Charles Darwin originated the theory of evolution. Actually, though, he didn't. Scientists have been trying to explain evolution since ancient times. Many of the early ideas were very different from Darwin's.

The ancient Greek philosophers Plato and Aristotle were the first to formulate these basic ideas. Plato believed that all the plants and animals on earth were reflections of "ideal" forms. All the different breeds of dogs, for example, reflected the ideal Dog; humans were the reflections of an ideal Human. Plato's student, Aristotle, believed that all the living things on earth could be arranged on a sort of "ladder of life," from the lowest (the fungi, such as molds and mushrooms) up through the higher plants, the primitive animals such as clams, crabs, and insects, and the higher animals, with humans at the very top.

The ideas of these Greek philosophers had influenced the way that people in Europe looked at the world. The traditions of the Judeo-Christian Bible were another major influence. As Christianity became the major religion throughout Europe, the two lines of thought were blended into the concept of **creationism**—that each species was created separately, in the same form in which it exists today. Dogs were always dogs; birds were always birds; and humans were always humans. Most supporters of creationism believe that the earth was created only thousands of years ago, rather than millions or billions of years ago as the theory of evolution requires.

✦ EARLY THEORIES ✦

For thousands of years, people firmly believed that living things could spring up overnight from nonliving things. The ancient Greeks thought that if wheat were allowed to rot in the barn, it would suddenly turn into mice. They believed that mud at the bottom of a pond could give rise to frogs, and that maggots and worms could come from rotting meat, in a kind of "spontaneous generation." After years of this traditional way of thinking, some scientists started to question the theory. The first serious challenge to creationism was made in 1668 by an Italian physician, Francesco Redi. Redi proved that maggots did not spontaneously appear in decaying meat, but from eggs laid there by flies.

In 1788 the Scottish geologist James Hutton published a theory that suggested that the earth was much older than the 6,000 years indicated in the Bible. Hutton also suggested that the earth was constantly changing, and that this was normal. Hutton's theory was supported by the English surveyor William Smith, who studied the layering of rocks and agreed that the earth was ancient. But Hutton's theory was not accepted by many of his colleagues.

In 1830 the English geologist Charles Lyell gave the final blow to creationism and laid the groundwork for modern geology. In his publication *Principles of Geology,* Lyell presented convincing evidence that slow, steady, natural change had been going on throughout the earth's history, and that this history extended over a long period of time—possibly millions of years.

Charles Darwin studied the theories of other scientists and incorpo-

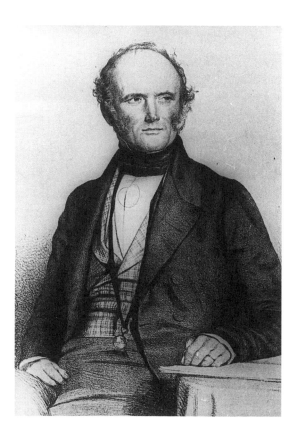

Geologist Charles Lyell (1797-1875)

rated many of their ideas into his own thoughts about evolution. Charles Lyell had a great influence on Darwin. Since Lyell suggested that the earth might be millions of years old, Darwin thought that if the earth's geological history changed over a long period of time, then perhaps it was possible that the living organisms on earth changed as well. Darwin believed this long time frame was essential for the gradual process involved in evolution.

Another important influence on Darwin was the English economist Thomas Malthus. In 1838 Darwin read an article that Malthus had written in 1798 titled *An Essay on the Principle of Population.* In the article, Malthus explained that as populations continue to reproduce, there would not be enough food to support the increasing organisms. This would cause a tremendous struggle for food and for existence in general.

But there is much individual variation among the members of any species, and even in a small, local population of a particular species. Darwin realized that some individuals had inherited variations of common traits that gave them an advantage in the "struggle for existence." These animals or plants would be better able to survive and to reproduce, and they would leave more offspring than the others. Since the particular traits that made them more successful are often hereditary, many of their offspring would have them too, and would be more successful in the fight for survival. Over the generations, the successful variations would become more and more common in the population. This realization became an important part of Darwin's theory of evolution.

✦ THE EVOLUTION OF DARWINISM ✦

Charles Darwin had been a naturalist since he was a child. He would gather specimens, classify them, and write up observations on what he found. In 1831, at twenty-two years of age, Charles Darwin was chosen for a five-year scientific expedition on the ship called the H.M.S. *Beagle.* The *Beagle* left Devonport, England, in late December 1831, and sailed down the west coast of Europe and Africa and up the west coast of South America. This route gave Darwin a chance to study plants, animals, fossils, and geological formations that no one had explored before. He also collected and categorized many samples of plants and animals from both coastal and inland areas, and wrote detailed notes in his journal.

The *Beagle* traveled to the Galápagos Islands, about 600 miles (965 km) off the coast of Ecuador, where it stayed for about five weeks. Darwin was amazed by the diversity of species compared to those of Europe. Darwin saw animal

Naturalist Charles Darwin (1809-1882) is pictured here surrounded by some of his drawings and notebooks from his voyage to the Galápagos Islands.

species on the islands that could not be found anywhere else on the earth. The islands were newly formed by volcanoes, long after the continents had formed. Therefore, the organisms found at the Galápagos Islands were either blown there by winds or floated there on ocean currents.

Among the various species, Darwin studied small birds called finches that were common on the islands. When he got back to England, Darwin realized that the Galápagos finches were closely related to each other and to a species of finch he had found on the west coast of South America. All the species of finches looked similar, but they had characteristics that reflected their specialized eating habits. For instance, the shape of their beaks differed depending on whether they were ground feeders, eating seeds and cacti, or fed on berries and insects in trees. Darwin's finches later became one of the important components in his theory of evolution.

In 1859 Charles Darwin introduced his theory of evolution in the best-selling book *On the Origin of Species by Means of Natural Selection.* Darwin used three vital sources in developing his theory: his personal observations, Charles Lyell's geological history of the earth, and the population theory offered by Thomas

Malthus. Darwin studied these ideas and theories and expanded them to formulate his own theory of evolution.

According to Darwin's theory of evolution, organisms that are best suited to the changing environment survive and produce more offspring. This process is called **natural selection**, which is also commonly referred to as "survival of the fittest."

Darwin's theory of natural selection was based on the following assumptions:

1. Individual organisms tend to produce more offspring than the environment can support. However, populations remain fairly stable in size because all members must compete for the available resources—there is a struggle for survival.

2. All members of populations have variations in their traits. The organisms with variations that are best suited to the environment survive. Variation must already be present in the population for natural selection to operate—it provides the raw materials for the process of evolution.

3. Organisms that survive pass on their favorable variations to their offspring by heredity. In time, these differences from the original population increase, and the individuals become so different from the original that they develop into a new species.

What a Coincidence!

In 1858, while completing the manuscript for a book on his theory of evolution, Charles Darwin received a brief essay about the same subject from the English naturalist Alfred Russel Wallace, who requested Darwin's opinion. To Darwin's surprise, Wallace had almost identical thoughts and ideas about evolution. Wallace had studied living organisms in the West Indies and came to the same conclusions as Darwin—that new species occur by natural selection.

Darwin considered withdrawing his manuscript; instead, with Wallace's approval, excerpts from both writings were read at a scientific meeting of the Linnaean Society in London in July 1858. Although both Darwin and Wallace developed the same basic ideas, Darwin's historic 1859 book *On the Origin of Species by Means of Natural Selection* captured the interest of the public and popularized his theory of evolution.

Although most scientists now support Darwin's idea of evolution, believers in traditional creationism kept a controversy stirred up for more than a century. The hottest arguments centered on the idea that not only plants and animals evolved into their present forms but humans, too, were the products of evolution rather than the highest creation of a Supreme Being. Believers in creationism could not accept the concept that we are "descended from the apes."

Can Evolution and Creationism Coexist?

In October 1996, Pope John Paul II acknowledged that evolution is "more than just a theory." Presently, the teaching of evolution is already a part of the curriculum in Roman Catholic schools. In the Pope's announcement, he gave support to the idea that it is possible for religious faith and the teaching of evolution in schools to coexist. The Pope asserted that the human soul was the result of immediate divine creation, but that scientific evidence seemed to point to the theory of evolution through natural selection.

Nonetheless, some other religions are still concerned about allowing evolution to be taught as fact rather than theory. In Alabama public schools, textbooks come with a disclaimer saying evolution is only one theory, not a fact. In Tennessee, teachers in many school districts say they do not teach evolution at all, to avoid becoming involved in the religious and political controversies.

The teaching of evolution in schools provoked bitter feelings. During the 1920's, laws in various places required teachers to teach only the biblical account of creation in public schools—how God created humans just as they are today. In 1925 John Thomas Scopes broke the law in Dayton, Tennessee, when he was caught teaching the theory of evolution in a high school. Scopes was brought to trial and found guilty of violating the Tennessee law that made teaching the theory of evolution in schools illegal. His conviction later was reversed because of a technicality. It was not until 1967 that the state legislature of Tennessee finally abolished the law.

John Thomas Scopes (seated, right) *was brought to trial in 1925 for teaching the theory of evolution in a Tennessee school. Even though he was defended by Clarence Darrow, a famous criminal lawyer, he was convicted and fined $100. His father is shown seated left.*

✦ THREE ✦

EVIDENCE FOR EVOLUTION

Did you ever look through your family photo album and notice that you have your grandmother's eyes or your uncle's nose? If you trace your family tree, you may find that you share similar characteristics with some of your relatives. It is true that we are all different—we look different, we sound different, we behave differently. But all members in a family, from generations past to the present, may share some similarities, such as the shape of the nose or the bone structure, for example. Fossil records provide a sort of "family album" for a number of species and are essential in determining the family history of a species.

✦ THE RECORD IN THE ROCKS ✦

Probably the most significant evidence for evolution comes from fossil records. The term *fossil* (from the Latin word *fossilis*, meaning "something dug up") refers to any evidence of ancient life. Ancient bones and teeth are among the most common fossils. They may be preserved when a dead animal becomes covered by sediments such as sand, silt, or mud. Soft tissues decay, but the harder skeleton remains. The sediments are deposited in layers, which gradually become pressed together into rocks, known as **sedimentary rocks**. Eventually, sedimentary rocks, such as sandstones, limestones, and shales, surround the animal remains. These fossils are brought to the surface by erosion or by digging. Fossils allow scientists to study the structure of ancient organisms, to compare them with existing life forms, and to speculate about the environment in which they existed. The fossil record also makes it possible to construct a time frame for the evolution of various life forms.

A fossil of a 150-million-year-old small dinosaur from the Jurassic Period

Fossils are rarely recovered in their entire form, but rather in bits and pieces that fit together like a puzzle. There are a variety of types of fossils. Many fossils consist of shells, skeletons, or teeth of animals, or the woody parts of plants. Other fossils include preserved footprints of animals that walked along a trail. Organisms may be buried in sediments where their remains are eventually changed into minerals, and they become petrified (turned to stone). Ancient insects have been preserved in amber, the hardened resin of certain types of trees. Other fossils were covered by tar or other natural preservatives, such as the liquid found in peat bogs. It is rare for the flesh and soft tissues of animals to be preserved. However, the frozen remains of mammoths have been found in

This crane fly has been preserved in amber for 38 million years.

Siberia and Alaska. In one instance, even the undigested contents of the mammoth's stomach were preserved. The mammoth fell into a crack in the ice more than 38,000 years ago.

TRACING THE FAMILY TREE

Although many fossils have been found, still more have yet to be recovered. Tracing the family tree is not easy for some species since there are gaps between time periods that would normally show how it evolved. People often complain that the fossil record has too many "missing links." Actually, considering how much has to go right for fossils to be formed at all, and then discovered, it is really amazing that we have as many as we do.

The horse does have a well-documented family history. Horses have been evolving over the past 60 million years. The earliest horse, known as *Eohippus* ("dawn horse"), was very small—only 10 to 20 inches (25 to 50 cm) high at the shoulder. It looked more like a dog than the horse we know today. Its front feet had four toes, and the back feet had three toes. Each toe had its own little hoof. These horses were browsers (leaf-eaters) and were well adjusted to the wooded areas where they lived.

As the environment changed, however, so did the horse. Over a long period of time, the horse's body changed; it became much taller—5 to 6 feet (1.5 to 1.8 meters) high—and its original four toes on the front feet and three on the back feet merged into one toe on each foot, with a single large hoof. The structure of the horse's teeth also changed, and the horse evolved into a grazer (grass-eater). The modern horse, *Equus,* is the product of millions of years of evolution.

One of the most striking fossil sites in the United States is at Rancho La Brea, in Los Angeles, California. Thousands of prehistoric animals have been trapped there in sticky pools of oil and asphalt, like flies glued to flypaper. Saber-tooth tigers, giant wolves, sloths, mastodons, bears, and horses have been recovered at Rancho La Brea.

The Grand Canyon in Arizona is a "geological history," written in stone. Some of the rocks in the deepest part of the Grand Canyon (a mile deep in some places) are 2 billion years old. Fossils found in the colorful layers of rock indicate that plants and animals had lived in the area millions of years ago.

✦ HOW DO WE DATE THE EARTH? ✦

Sedimentary rocks preserve many fossils. As the minerals in the rocks are deposited over time, the more recent layers are on top of the older, earlier ones. Therefore, it is usually possible to distinguish the older fossils from the more recent ones just by observing the layers where they are found. However, in some cases the layering may have been disturbed by folding and faulting. This is taken into consideration when determining the age of certain fossils.

Stratigraphy is the study of the earth's strata, or rock layers. By studying the sequences of rock layers in different areas, stratigraphers can match up a particular geologic event to a particular time period. Stratigraphy can show the sequence of events—which animal species lived before which other ones, for example—but it does not tell us exactly when these events occurred. Scientists cannot tell a fossil's age just by looking at it. Laboratory tests are needed for this.

The chemical elements that make up rocks and fossils are actually a mixture of forms, called **isotopes**. Most of each element is made up of stable isotopes, which always stay the same, but a small proportion consists of radioactive isotopes. These chemicals give off invisible rays and are very gradually converted to isotopes of a different element. For example, one radioactive isotope of uranium (U-235) decays over time into lead (Pb-207). This radioactive decay occurs at a definite rate for each isotope and can be measured with a Geiger counter or some other instrument sensitive to radiations. From the proportions of different isotopes present in a sample of rock, scientists can calculate how long its radioisotopes have been decaying—that is, how old it is.

The time it takes for one-half of a radioisotope to change into a different material is known as its **half-life**. The half-lives of different radioisotopes vary enormously. For example, the half-life of one isotope of iodine (I-232) is only 2.4 hours, while the half-life of the uranium isotope U-235 is 704 million years.

Several different radioisotopes are used in dating fossils. These include potassium (K-40, half-life 1.3 billion years), uranium (U-235, half-life 704 million years); and carbon (C-14, half-life 5,730 years). Because of its relatively short half-life, carbon-14 is useful for dating fossils that are 50,000 years old or less. In contrast, postassium-40, with its long half-life, can be used to date fossils that are hundreds of millions of years old. Wherever possible, the age of a fossil is tested independently, using two or more different isotopes.

✦ STILL ADAPTING ✦

According to the theory of evolution, organisms have developed various **adaptations** in order to adjust to a changing environment. During most of the earth's history, the environmental changes have occurred in gradual stages. Beginning in the 1800s, however, the environment started to change at a much faster rate—and so did evolution. The natural habitats of many plants and animals have been changed or destroyed as the human population continues to grow. These changing habitats have led to new adaptations. Observations of these adaptations have supported the theory of evolution.

The peppered moth is a good example of an organism that went through rapid evolution in response to environmental changes. Originally, almost all peppered moths that lived in industrial areas of Great Britain were white with black spots. The population also included a few moths that were completely black. The light-colored moths were able to blend in with the trunks of certain trees, but the black ones were easily spotted by birds, which ate them. The black moths thus were less likely to survive long enough to have offspring; natural selection was operating to keep their proportion in the population small. During the mid-1800's, however, soot from the new factories started to blacken the bark of many trees. The light-colored moths were now more visible to the birds than the black ones. Many light-colored moths were eaten, and their numbers declined greatly. The black moths, on the other hand, now had an advantage in the struggle for survival. Birds were less likely to spot them against the black tree trunks. The black variation quickly became common and widespread.

✦ GEOGRAPHY LESSON ✦

Why are some plants and animals found only in certain regions? The theory of evolution provides an explanation for the geographic distribution of species. When a species evolved in one place, it multiplied until it was stopped by an environmental obstacle, such as an ocean, a change in climate, or a scarcity of food. For instance, giraffes and zebras cannot be found in the wild outside Africa, and certain types of monkeys live only in South America. Australian mammals are an extreme example of the isolated evolution of species. The Australian continent was separated from the rest of the world when mammals evolved into most of their present forms. That is why kangaroos, koalas, and other species in Australia cannot be found anywhere else in the world. It is also the reason that Australia does not have many of the animals that live on the other continents.

✦ COMPARING ANATOMY ✦

A wide variety of animals exist all over the world. They may be as large as an elephant or as small as a mouse, and their lifestyles may differ greatly. Birds have wings for flying and strong claws to grasp objects like branches or tools; fish have fins adapted for swimming; and horses have sturdy legs that allow them to run across rough terrain. Linnaeus had classified species by their outward appearance, but the French scientist Georges Cuvier decided that species should be classified by their internal structure. Cuvier realized that despite the apparent differences between animals, they actually shared similarities in their internal structure. Similarities in the bones inside the forelimbs of birds and mammals, for instance, might suggest that they evolved from a common ancestor. Through evolution, their limbs have been modified to adapt to a

Koalas are one of the species that evolved in an isolated environment. They are marsupials and are found in the wild only in Australia.

specific function. These similar internal structures are called **homologous structures**.

Comparative anatomy allows scientists to study the relationships between organisms. They theorize that the more similar the internal structures of two species are, the more closely related they must be and the more recently they must have strayed from a common ancestor.

✦ CHEMICALS OF LIFE ✦

Biochemistry—the study of the chemicals that make up living organisms—gives additional evidence that all the living things on our planet are related. All plants, animals, and even microscopic creatures such as bacteria and viruses store their operating instructions and the blueprints for making more of their species in chemicals called nucleic acids (DNA and RNA). They all use basically the same "code" to spell out these instructions and build proteins from the same set of twenty kinds of simpler building blocks, called amino acids.

The great similarities in the basic chemicals of all organisms show that they are related, but there are variations. The kinds and amounts of these chemical differences show *how* they are related. Animals and plants whose proteins or nucleic acids are very similar are very closely related; those with more differences are more distant relatives.

Our biochemistry reveals how closely humans are related to the monkeys and apes—close to 99 percent of the DNA in our genes is the same as the genetic information of chimpanzees! The other 1 percent has produced quite a few differences, though, and took a long time to evolve: Scientists have calculated from comparisons of DNA that our ancestors branched off from the line that produced chimpanzees about 5 million years ago.

✦ EMBRYOS TELL THE TALE ✦

Chickens, pigs, fish, and humans look quite different from one another, but would you believe these organisms all start out looking almost exactly the same? In the 1800s an Estonian biologist, Karl von Baer, realized that all **vertebrates** (animals with backbones) look like one another in certain stages of their early development. For example, fish, turtles, chickens, mice, and humans all develop fishlike tails and gills during the **embryo** stage, early in their development before birth. However, only fish continue to develop gills, and only fish, turtles, and mice keep the tails.

Why would vertebrates that grow up to be so different be so similar in their early developmental stages? Scientists theorize that these organisms may come from a common ancestor that had genes determining the development of gills and tails. These genes are passed on to the descendants. In fish, these genes are "turned on" throughout development, leading to the formation of gills and tails in the adults. In humans and chickens, however, these genes are "turned on" only in the embryos; as they develop further, these genes are "turned off," and the gills and tails disappear.

✦ ARTIFICIAL SELECTION ✦

Evolution is not always a natural process. For thousands of years, farmers have been controlling evolution by breeding plants and domestic animals to produce offspring with specific desirable traits. Offspring with harmful traits would not be used for reproductive purposes. This process is called **artificial selection**. In this process, farmers can use artificial selection to produce corn with the biggest ears or plants with the hardiest flowers. Dog breeding is probably the best example of artificial selection. Over the last few thousand years, breeders have produced the large variety of dogs we have today.

After observing artificial selection, Darwin realized that selection over a long period of time could bring about major changes within a species. This led to his formulation of the concept of natural selection.

✦ FOUR ✦

How Evolution Works

What would happen if all members of a species were exactly the same—they all looked the same, they all acted the same, they all had the same genetic makeup? If that were possible, natural selection could not exist. No members of the species would have any special advantages in the struggle for existence; chance alone would determine which ones would survive and leave offspring, and the outcome would not matter since all the offspring would be the same. But what if there were then a change in the environment? Perhaps the weather got cooler, or a dam diverted a stream, making some areas drier and flooding others. Perhaps the species could survive under the new conditions, or perhaps it could not. If all the members of the species were the same, they might all die out.

Variation is a species' insurance, a defense against future changes. Some of the diverse individuals in a natural population might not be the best adapted to the particular conditions of the present—like the few black moths in the English peppered moth population before industry blackened the tree trunks. But as long as some of them were around, they might save their species if the environment changed. According to Darwin and Wallace, heredity is essential in evolution—traits are passed from one generation to another, which allows for variation. At the time the theory of evolution was proposed, however, no one knew exactly how heredity worked.

✦ CAN ACQUIRED CHARACTERISTICS BE INHERITED? ✦

In 1801 the French scientist Jean-Baptiste Lamarck became one of the first to suggest a mechanism for evolution. In Lamarck's view, when an organism adapted to environmental changes, it acquired new characteristics that could be passed on to its offspring. For example, Lamarck explained that ancient giraffes developed their characteristic long neck by stretching to feed on leaves on the higher branches of trees. Their offspring inherited these longer necks, and soon stretched even farther to reach leaves on even higher branches. Eventually, this evolutionary process would produce modern giraffes with very long necks.

When Lamarck studied the fossil record, he noticed that the older fossils were much simpler, while the more recent fossils were more complex and more similar to modern-day organisms. This observation helped Lamarck to formulate a theory of evolution:

1. A characteristic may be acquired through use or lost through disuse.
2. An acquired or lost characteristic may be passed from one generation to the next.
3. During evolution, the form of the characteristic becomes more and more complex as it evolves.

At that time, nothing was known about genetics, so Lamarck's theory seemed reasonable. Charles Darwin's grandfather, Erasmus Darwin, also supported the idea that the offspring of organisms inherited acquired characteristics. However, scientists now know that acquired characteristics cannot be inherited. Only the genes—the DNA of sex cells—can be passed from parents to their offspring. Lamarck's studies, however, were helpful to Darwin when he formulated his theory of evolution.

✦ GENETICS: THE MISSING LINK IN DARWIN'S THEORY ✦

Charles Darwin believed that in order for natural selection to occur, members of a species must pass on their traits to the next generation. However, it was not until nearly two decades after Darwin's death that scientists learned about the principles of genetics.

In the mid-1800s an Austrian monk named Gregor Mendel had conducted experiments on peas in his monastery garden in what later became Brno, Czechoslovakia. Growing thousands of seeds and carefully recording the characteristics of the plants and seeds in each generation, Mendel formulated some basic principles of genetics. He published an article in 1865, in the journal of the local natural-science society, but practically nobody read it. Then, in an amazing

Botanist Gregor Mendel
(1822-1884)

coincidence, three different researchers independently worked out the principles of genetics, discovered Mendel's article in 1900, and called the attention of the scientific community to his work.

In the 1920s Darwin's theory of evolution was modified to include an explanation of the genetic aspect of natural selection. Darwin's theory, Mendelian genetics, and other genetic advances were combined to form a more complete explanation of evolution known as neo-**Darwinism** or the synthetic theory of evolution.

Gregor Mendel and the biologists who expanded on his work discovered that chemical units called **genes** determine traits that are passed from one generation to another. An organism has two copies of the gene for each trait—one from its mother and one from its father. That is why an offspring can look different from its parents but share similar characteristics.

Each time a set of traits is passed on from one generation to the next, it is like dealing a new hand from a well-shuffled deck of cards. Each offspring gets a complete set of genes, but which gene in a particular pair it receives from its mother and which one is received from its father is determined by chance.

In each pair of genes, one may be **dominant** (the variation of the trait that it produces will always appear, no matter what kind of gene is paired with it) and the other may be **recessive** (the variation it produces will not show unless the offspring happens to receive two of that particular gene). For example, some of Mendel's peas produced green seeds and some produced yellow ones. The yellow seeds always produced plants with yellow seeds, but those with green seeds, when crossed with green-seed plants, gave mostly offspring with green seeds but a few with yellow ones. Mendel deduced that yellow seed color was a recessive trait, showing up only in plants with two genetic units for yellow; a green seed color was a dominant trait, which was expressed even in plants with a mixed pair of genes, one green and one yellow.

The inheritance of blue and brown eyes in humans works in a similar way (brown is dominant, and blue is a recessive trait). But other genes can also affect the expression of this human trait—so some people have green or gray or hazel eyes instead of blue or brown.

The reshuffling of genes that occurs during sexual reproduction is enough to provide a great deal of variation in a population, but there is another source that can actually give rise to brand-new traits. Sometimes genes may change, or mutate. **Mutations** may occur while the genes are being copied, during the formation of the sex cells. A mutated gene causes a variation in an individual trait. If the variation is positive, it will help the organism survive and will be more likely to be passed on to the next generation. If the variation is harmful, however, the organism has a reduced chance of survival. Most mutations are either harmful or make no particular difference to the organism. Helpful mutations are rare. But when they do occur, natural selection may operate to make them more common in the local population of the species. Eventually this process may produce a new species.

There is a variety of hair and eye color among the children in this family, showing that the genes inherited from the parents can be expressed in different ways.

✦ THE DEVELOPMENT OF A NEW SPECIES ✦

According to Darwin, the development of a new species, or **speciation**, was "the gradual accumulation of changes in ancestry over time, until the group was distinct enough to be considered a new species." Many biologists believe speciation occurs once a species has been separated into two or more **isolated** populations. Through natural selection, these isolated populations adapt to changing environments and develop different traits. Over time, the populations become so diverse that the members of one group cannot breed successfully with those of another. Thus, speciation has occurred.

What causes populations to become isolated? Isolation may be geographic, ecological, or genetic.

Geographic isolation may occur when groups of organisms are separated by deserts, islands, mountains, and oceans. Members of the species, therefore, may live in different geographical locations and become adapted to different climates, habitats, and lifestyles.

Ecological isolation occurs when populations live in different habitats within in the same general area. Some members may have specialized adaptations to fit their lifestyle. For instance, birds that eat nuts and seeds may have a stronger beak than those that drink nectar from flowers. Eventually, the members with specialized adaptations may form a new distinct species.

Genetic isolation occurs when mutations affect sexual traits. Organisms with these mutations may be able to breed with each other, but not with other members of the species. Eventually, their descendants form separate species. Different plant species may produce flowers at different times of the year, so that pollen from the flowers of one species never has a chance to fertilize the flowers of another species growing in the same field. Sometimes the **chromosomes** (the structures formed by groups of genes) of two related species have become so different that they do not match up correctly when the sex cells are forming. So matings between individuals of two species can occur, but then there can be no "next generation" to inherit their traits.

✦ PATTERNS OF EVOLUTION ✦

As new species form over time and adapt to their changing environments through natural selection, different patterns of evolution may develop. The most common pattern is **divergent evolution**. This occurs when two or more species evolve from a common ancestor and then become increasingly different over time, such as monkeys and apes, which diverged from a common ancestor but are now different species. DNA studies have revealed some surprising relationships among very different-seeming species. Elephants, for example, have been found to be fairly close relatives of "sea cows," or manatees. The manatees

The aquatic manatee bears little resemblance to its relative the elephant, except in skin color.

developed a more streamlined body and flipperlike limbs as they changed from land mammals to sea-dwellers.

Another pattern of evolution is **convergent evolution**. In convergent evolution, even though species have different ancestors, they may look similar to one another and have similar adaptations. Birds, bats, and butterflies are examples of this. All have wings, but their ancestors independently developed this adaptation for flying, and the internal structure of the wings is markedly different. The mammals of Australia show striking similarities to various kinds of mammals in the rest of the world, even though their common ancestors were separated about 100 million years ago when Australia split off from the other continents. Thus, there are marsupial "mice" and "cats" that look and act much like the mice and cats in Eurasia and the Americas. The egg-laying echidnas (spiny anteaters) of Australia and New Guinea, the aardvarks of Africa, and the anteaters of the tropical Americas all developed a long, tapered snout and a long tongue used for probing anthills.

✦ FIVE ✦

THE HISTORY OF LIFE ON EARTH

For centuries, scientists have been trying to answer the burning question. "How did life begin?" In the 1920s and 1930s, Aleksandr Oparin in Russia and J.B.S. Haldane in England provided their own speculations. Although the spontaneous generation theory, which suggests that living organisms rise from nonliving matter, had been laid to rest, Oparin and Haldane thought that if the conditions are right, life could have emerged from nonliving matter through a gradual process of **chemical evolution**. Over time, simple organic molecules combined spontaneously to form increasingly complex organic compounds.

✦ THE GEOLOGICAL TIME SCALE ✦

Evolution is often a very gradual process; the changes are small, accumulating over a long period of time. By studying the rock strata and their fossils, scientists have created a kind of timeline that names each period in the earth's history, gives its approximate time span, and describes the organisms that were in existence during that time. There are five main **eras**: Archeozoic, Proterozoic, Paleozoic, Mesozoic, and Cenozoic. Each era marks the beginning or ending of a significant geological or biological event, such as the mass **extinction** of a species. The Proterozoic, Paleozoic, and Mesozoic eras are subdivided into periods, which indicate less dramatic biological events. The most recent era, the

Cenozoic, is subdivided even further into **epochs**. Geological time covers enormous spans of years, far longer than we normally think—thousands, millions, and even billions of years.

✦ THE BIRTH OF THE EARTH ✦

About 4.6 billion years ago, rocks came crashing together as the earth started to form. The energies of motion were converted into heat. As radioactive materials in the rocks decayed, even more heat was released. Soon the earth became so hot that the rocks melted, and heavy elements, such as iron and nickel, sank to the center of the earth and formed the earth's core. Less dense materials, such as silicates (rocks made largely of silicon and oxygen) floated to the surface and formed the earth's crust. Other chemicals had also risen to the surface—some formed water (oxygen combined with hydrogen), and others formed the gases in the atmosphere. Over millions of years, the earth cooled enough so that the water turned into a liquid and rained over the land to form oceans. The rainwater dissolved minerals from the rocks and made the oceans salty. Scientists refer to the time during which the earth was forming as the Archeozoic Era.

The earth's early atmosphere was probably filled with the gases methane, ammonia, nitrogen, hydrogen, and water vapor, along with small amounts of carbon dioxide and sulfur compounds. But what about oxygen? Today, almost all living things need oxygen to live. But when the earth was young, all the oxygen was already bonded in water, carbon dioxide, and other minerals. So there was no free oxygen in the atmosphere, and therefore, organisms that depended on oxygen to live could not exist.

✦ THE FIRST SIGNS OF LIFE ✦

The first living cells probably appeared on the earth about 3.5 billion years ago, at the end of the **Archeozoic Era**. (*Archeozoic* comes from Greek words meaning "ancient life.") They most likely were single-celled creatures that must have been able to live without oxygen, since there was no oxygen gas in the atmosphere, nor any dissolved in the sea. These living cells were primitive **anaerobic** bacteria. (*Anaerobic* means "living without oxygen.") These primitive organisms consumed many kinds of organic molecules, such as sugars and amino acids, the building blocks of proteins. By breaking down the energy-rich compounds through a process called **fermentation,** in which oxygen was not needed, they got the nutrients and energy that they needed to live.

As these ancient bacteria multiplied, they used up their food supply of organic molecules. Mutations occurred, and some cells were able to obtain energy directly from the sunlight. They no longer needed the energy-rich compounds that were now in short supply in the environment. These organisms became the first **autotrophs**—organisms that use the sun's energy to produce their own food from simple raw materials by a process called **photosynthesis**. The appearance of such more-complex single-celled creatures marked the end of the Archeozoic Era and the beginning of the **Proterozoic Era**, about 2.5 billion years ago. (*Proterozoic* comes from Greek words meaning "earlier life.") Some scientists refer to the two eras as the **Precambrian Time**. Together, they cover about 80 percent of the earth's history.

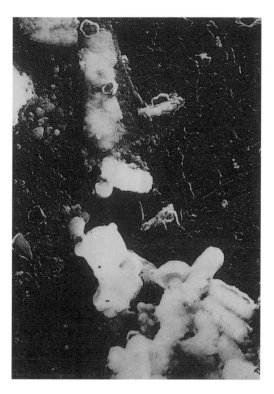

These bacteria microfossils are about 2 million years old. Bacteria developed on the earth about 3.5 billion years ago.

If autotrophs had never emerged, life might have ended with the anaerobic bacteria. The autotrophs not only provided food for themselves, but they were an important food source for **heterotrophs**—organisms that feed on other organisms for food. The first photosynthetic autotrophs produced food from hydrogen-rich molecules like hydrogen sulfide (H_2S), releasing sulfur (not oxygen) in the process.

The first photosynthetic autotrophs to split water (H_2O) in order to obtain hydrogen were the cyanobacteria. Water was a plentiful raw material on the young earth, so these single-celled organisms thrived and multiplied. During photosynthesis, the cyanobacteria used the energy from the sun to convert water and carbon dioxide into organic compounds, such as sugars, starches, and other carbohydrates. As a result, oxygen (O_2) was released as a gas. Eventually, oxygen started to accumulate in the oceans and atmosphere.

The increase in oxygen in the atmosphere had a serious impact on living organisms. Oxygen was poisonous to the anaerobes, and many species most likely died. Some were able to survive in places like cracks in the deep-sea bottom, where oxygen did not penetrate. Other organisms, called **aerobes**, developed ways to make oxygen less harmful or even useful. They developed a process called respiration, which used the oxygen to get energy from food. Their appearance marked the end of the Proterozoic Era and the beginning of the **Paleozoic Era**. (*Paleozoic* comes from Greek words meaning "old life.")

✦ THE FIRST ANIMALS ✦

The first animals emerged when groups of living cells came together to form colonies. The individual cells helped each other to make or gather food. Mutations occurred in some of them, and they became specialized—some gathered food, others reproduced, and others had specialized structures for moving around. Specialization had advantages—the organisms as a whole could do more things more efficiently—but the individual cells could no longer survive on their own.

Trilobites were common 500 million years ago. Most of these prehistoric sea creatures were under 4 inches (10 cm) long. They breathed through gills on their legs.

As the animals started to get bigger and more complex, they needed a protective outer covering. The first type of animals were **invertebrates** (animals without backbones). Some animals, such as worms and jellyfish, had soft bodies. Other animals, such as snails and starfish, had hard outer shells. These shells also served as skeletons, to which muscles could be attached for more efficient movements. **Arthropods** (animals with "jointed legs"), which included the trilobites, were the largest group of invertebrates. These animals were the ancestors of today's insects, crabs, shrimp, and spiders. Almost all types of invertebrates had evolved by the end of the Cambrian Period, about 480 million years ago. All animals still lived in the sea at that time.

The last type of prehistoric animals to evolve were **vertebrates**. Vertebrates had advantages over the invertebrates.

The skeleton of a vertebrate was inside its body, and it was much lighter to carry around than an outer skeleton. Vertebrates also had more mobility. Some of the first vertebrates that appeared were fish without jaws or teeth. Jawless fish ate by sucking up little pieces of dead animals along the ocean floor. About 420 million years ago, fish with jaws evolved; they could attack and eat larger animals. They could also move around more easily than jawless fish. About 405 million years ago, during the Devonian Period, there were so many kinds of fish that it is often called the Age of Fishes.

✦ MOVING ONTO LAND ✦

During the middle of the Paleozoic Era, about 425 million years ago, plants became the first living organisms to appear on land. These included scale trees, scouring rushes, and ferns. They were an important food source for animals that came later. The first land invertebrates were arthropods, which included insects and spiders. Living on land was a major adjustment. They had to use lungs for breathing instead of gills, and they needed a circulatory system to carry oxygen throughout the body. They also had to support the weight of their bodies against gravity because they no longer had the cushion of the water.

About 400 million years ago, the first vertebrates to live on land were amphibians, ancestors of today's salamanders, frogs, and toads. The ancient amphibians had heads and tails like fish, but they had short feet and could stay out of water for long periods of time. They returned to the water to lay their eggs.

Then, about 310 million years ago, some amphibians evolved into lizardlike creatures, known as reptiles. An important difference from their amphibian ancestors was that reptiles could lay their eggs on land. Reptiles were therefore more active on land than amphibians. Toward the end of the Paleozoic Era, seas dried up and deserts spread over large areas. Many amphibians died as the climate changed. But the reptiles adjusted to the warmer and drier climates. By the start of the **Mesozoic Era**, about 225 million years ago, the reptiles dominated the land, sea, and air. The Age of Reptiles, as it is commonly called, lasted for 160 million years. Some common reptiles included crocodiles, lizards, snakes, and turtles.

The most extraordinary reptiles during the Mesozoic Era were the dinosaurs. (The term *dinosaur* comes from two Greek words meaning "terrible lizard.") The dinosaurs varied greatly—some were as small as chickens and others were enormous. The brachiosaurs were among the largest known dinosaurs, measuring about 80 feet (24 meters) in length—as long as two buses in a row. They were not predators; they ate only plants. They did have to watch out for the fierce meat-eating dinosaurs, such as *Tyrannosaurus rex*. The dinosaurs became extinct by the end of the Mesozoic Era.

Flying reptiles and giant sea reptiles also became extinct by the end of the Mesozoic Era, but smaller reptiles such as crocodiles, lizards, snakes, and turtles survived into modern times. Other organisms also survived the mass extinction: Invertebrates, such as lobsters, crabs, and shrimp, continued to evolve during the Mesozoic Era, as did the first bony fish.

Birds evolved during the Mesozoic Era, probably from dinosaurs. The first birds had feathers that trapped a layer of air close to their bodies and kept them warm even in very cold temperatures. Later, some primitive birds developed longer, stronger feathers on their forelimbs, which allowed them to glide from trees. Birds that could fly evolved from these gliders. In early 1998, Chinese researchers described the discovery northeast of Beijing of dinosaur fossils with featherlike features along the neck, back, and tail. The fossils, about 145 million years old, may help to fill a gap in the fossil record between dinosaurs and birds.

WHAT HAPPENED TO THE DINOSAURS?

Imagine an enormous asteroid, about 6 to 12 miles (10 to 20 km) across, crashing into the earth. Dust clouds from the asteroid fill the air and become so thick that light from the sun is blocked all over the planet. The earth is dark and cold. The plants soon die, and so do the plant-eating animals. Eventually, the meat-eaters also die because their food source has disappeared. Some scientists believe that this "asteroid theory" explains how the dinosaurs became extinct 65 million years ago.

The asteroid theory faced a lot of criticism when it was first introduced in 1980. Many critics preferred to stick to the traditional thinking that the mass extinction was a long, gradual process brought on by volcanic eruptions, which polluted the atmosphere and changed the climate. Others suggested that the mass extinction was caused by huge bursts of cosmic rays, high-energy particles that travel through space between the stars.

Since 1980, scientists have continued to collect evidence indicating that an impact, whether an asteroid or comet, did occur during the late Cretaceous Period. A huge crater, named Chicxulub, has been discovered buried beneath the northern tip of Mexico's Yucatán peninsula. Rock strata in the Chicxulub date from 65 million years, about the time that the dinosaurs became extinct.

A fossilized sea turtle skeleton from the late Cretaceous Period. This turtle lived at the time of the dinosaurs.

Mammals first appeared during the Mesozoic Era. They evolved from small reptiles. The first mammals were about the size of rats, with furry bodies and pointed snouts. Like birds' feathers, the hair of mammals provided insulation against the cold. Unlike birds, however, which still laid eggs like their reptilian ancestors, mammals gave birth to live young. One group of early mammals, the **monotremes**, were an exception: They laid eggs but—like modern mammals—fed their babies with milk produced in special mammary glands on the mother's belly. Only a few kinds of monotremes survive today: the duckbilled platypus and the echidna, "living fossils" that are found mainly on the Australian continent.

Australia is also the main refuge for another kind of early mammals, the **marsupials**. These mammals give birth to young that are not really finished developing. The offspring then crawl into a pouch on their mother's abdomen and continue to develop by drinking milk from her nipples. Australia and New Zealand have a great variety of native marsupials, including kangaroos, koalas, wallabies, and many other species. The only marsupials living wild on other continents today are the opossums.

Placental mammals evolved after the marsupials. They provide their unborn young with nourishment inside the mother's body through an organ called the placenta. They give birth to young that are more fully developed; in fact, some young placental mammals are able to walk only a few hours after birth. Placentals dominated the next era in history, called the Cenozoic Era or the Age of Mammals.

At the start of the **Cenozoic Era**, about 65 million years ago, the early mammals were very small. An ancestor of the elephant, for instance, was about the size of a pig and did not have a trunk and tusks. As the mammals evolved, some remained small, while others grew larger. The larger size allowed for the development of bigger and more-complex brains, which could cope with the more-varied challenges of life on land. A growing diversity of mammals spread out into all the land habitats, from deserts to swamps and rain forests. Some mammals eventually returned to a life in the sea, streamlining their bodies and acquiring a fishlike shape through convergent evolution.

SIX

THE EVOLUTION OF US

Would you believe that you are related to tiny, insect-eating, tree-dwelling shrews? These mammals were the earliest **primates**, and they looked very much like tiny mice. When scientists first announced that humans evolved from primates, people were frightened at the thought that we descended from the apes. What a blow to a person's ego—from being the center of the universe to the grandchild of a monkey! But that is not completely accurate. There are no currently living species of monkeys or apes that are direct ancestors of humans. Instead, we share a common ancestor from millions of years ago.

✦ PRIMATE EVOLUTION ✦

Fossil records indicate that primitive tree shrews lived about 65 million years ago. Soon after this primate line began, it split into two major groups of primates. The first group, called the **prosimians** (meaning "before monkeys"), or "lower primates," evolved from the primitive tree shrews. The prosimians resembled the present-day tarsiers and lemurs.

The second group, the **anthropoids** (meaning "humanlike") or "higher primates," included monkeys, apes, and humans. The anthropoids split into two groups as a result of geological changes that caused the continents of Africa and South America to drift away from one another. The New World monkeys of

Central and South America had long tails that could grasp things almost like an extra hand, which helped them to swing from trees. The Old World monkeys of Asia and Africa either lacked tails or had nongrasping tails.

After the continents drifted apart, another split occurred among the Old World anthropoids. The great apes branched off from the monkeys. (No apes evolved in the New World.) These apes are called **hominoids**, which means "resembling or related to humans." They include the gibbons and orangutans of Asia and the gorillas and chimpanzees of Africa. These great apes are the largest primates, and there is a noticeable increase in skull size and brain development compared with the Old World and New World monkeys. In addition, the apes not only look similar to humans, but studies of their anatomy and laboratory tests indicate that they are our closest relatives. Scientists have found that chimpanzees, for instance, are more closely related to humans than they are to gorillas.

Gibbons are the smallest of the apes, growing only to about 3 feet (91 cm) tall. They live mainly in the tree tops and walk upright from branch to branch.

From the primitive tree shrews to the prosimians to the anthropoids, primates have gradually changed, adapting to their new lifestyles. Early primates were nocturnal, but over time many became active during the day. Many primates stayed in trees, while some, such as the baboons, became ground-dwellers. There was also a progressive shortening of the snout and an improvement of the focusing of the eyes. Their teeth became modified for an omnivorous diet of both plant and animal foods. There was also a significant increase in brain size throughout primate evolution.

LIFE IN TREES

Before the separate lines of primates split off, they evolved certain adaptations to life in trees:

- Their eyes moved to the front of the head, giving them excellent binocular (three-dimensional) vision. This provided good depth perception, so they could judge the distances between trees as they swung from branch to branch. Scientists believe that they also had color vision.
- Their hands and feet had five digits (fingers and toes), including an opposable thumb that could swing around to meet the fingers in a firm or delicate grip. Their long, grasping fingers could easily hold onto the branches of trees, zip open a banana to eat, or pluck tiny parasites out of each other's fur.
- Scientists think that primates' unusually large brains may have evolved along with their skills; their binocular color vision, quick movement through trees, and agility with their hands would require a lot of brainpower.

✦ ALMOST HUMAN ✦

Scientists believe that the earliest humanlike primates appeared no more than 5 to 7 million years ago. Considering that the first signs of life appeared billions of years ago, the arrival of humans is really a short time ago in geological history. Think in terms of a 24-hour time period. Imagine that the earth formed at midnight, life appeared at 8:20 A.M., the first vertebrates appeared at 9:35 P.M., and the first humans emerged only 2 minutes before midnight. In the last "2 minutes" of the earth's history, humans have evolved from primates with some humanlike features to the modern humans we know today.

The first humanlike primates, or **hominids**, were the Australopithecines ("southern apes") that lived in Africa. These hominids were almost human—but not quite. Australopithecines were ground-dwellers that stood only 3.5 to 4.5 feet (107 to 137 cm) tall and weighed only 40 to 50 pounds (18 to 23 kg).

Their physical structure was apelike, with a long upper body and arms but short legs. Their faces were apelike, too, with a low forehead sloping down to heavy eyebrow ridges and a forward-jutting jaw with apelike teeth. There was not much room for a brain inside the heavy skull: The Australopithecines had a very small brain with a capacity of only 450 to 500 cubic centimeters (28 to 30 cubic inches), compared with a modern human brain capacity of 1400 cubic centimeters (85 cubic inches). However, the head sat on top of the backbone like a human's rather than projecting forward like an ape's, and the bones in the hands were like those of humans (but with chimpanzeelike joints). Fossil footprints indicate that the legs, feet, and hips of Australopithecines were positioned for walking fully upright on two legs. This shows that an upright two-legged posture was the first major human trait to evolve, long before a large brain or the use of tools.

LUCY IN THE SKY WITH DIAMONDS

In 1974 anthropologist Donald Johanson of the Cleveland Museum of Natural History made a historic discovery. In search of hominid fossils, Johanson traveled to a remote area in Ethiopia. He got lucky when he found the skeleton of a very primitive, small-brained female hominid who was only 3.5 feet (107 cm) tall. This was the best-preserved human skeleton ever found—about 40 percent complete. The skeleton showed that hominids had walked erect. On the night of the discovery, Johanson and his associates had a party to celebrate the find. Johanson named this primitive hominid "Lucy" because the Beatles' song "Lucy in the Sky with Diamonds" was played at the party. Lucy is an excellent illustration of the transition from apes to humans.

✦ THE FIRST HUMANS ✦

About 2.4 million years ago, the human genus ***Homo,*** or true "man," emerged. Some scientists believe that the connecting link between Australopithecines and the first true humans was the emergence of *Homo habilis* ("handy man"). *Homo* *habilis* walked upright and stood about 5 feet (152 cm) tall, making them larger than Australopithecines. *Homo habilis* was also more intelligent than the Australopithecines, with a brain capacity of about 700 cubic centimeters (43 cubic inches). Fossils of *Homo habilis* have been found in various sites in Africa, along with some primitive tools. Although other primates often used tools, *Homo habilis* is considered to be the first species to actually create them. Some hunters probably used these tools to kill animals for food. Their meat-eating habits separated *Homo habilis* from all earlier hominids and hominoids, which had a primarily vegetarian diet. The use of tools and tool-making skills became dominant in the rest of human evolution.

About 1.7 million years ago, a new species, *Homo erectus* ("erect man"), emerged. *Homo habilis* had stayed in areas from northeastern to southern Africa, but *Homo erectus* traveled from northern Africa to southern Asia into Indonesia, and also to southern Europe. In 1985 a nearly complete skeleton was discovered in northern Kenya, Africa. The fossils showed that it was a twelve-year-old boy whose features still looked more similar to his ape ancestors than to modern man.

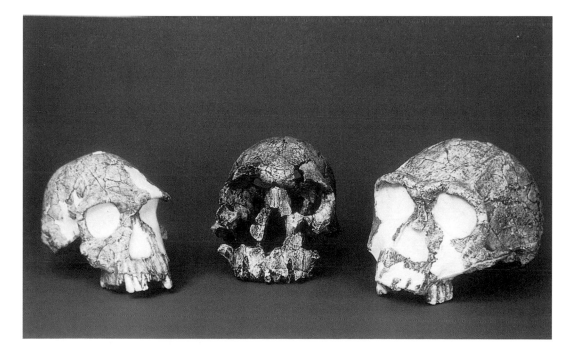

A comparison (left to right) *of the skulls of* Australopithecus africanus, Homo habilis, *and* Homo erectus

After close examination, scientists could tell that the species *Homo erectus* walked completely upright, and the boy would have grown to 6 feet (183 cm) tall as an adult. The brain capacity, about 800 cubic centimeters (49 cubic inches), was larger than that of *Homo habilis*. The increased intelligence of *Homo erectus* resulted in their making more sophisticated tools, such as hand axes, and possibly choppers, borers, and scrapers. Some hunters used these tools to kill big-game animals, such as elephants, bears, and antelope. *Homo erectus* was the first group of hominids to wear clothes, build fires, and live in caves and shelters so they could survive in areas where the weather was cold.

THE SEARCH FOR MOTHER EVE

The science of genetics usually deals with the inheritance of genes carried on chromosomes, structures found inside the nucleus of each cell. But each of our cells also carries another, independent set of genes, in structures called mitochondria. The **mitochondria** are the cell's energy generators. The sex cells, egg and sperm, have mitochondria, but when they join to form a new individual, only the chromosomes of the sperm enter the egg; its mitochondria do not. So each of us inherits a set of mitochondrial genes that came only from our mother, none from our father. Moreover, except for mutations, it is the same set of mitochondrial genes that came from her mother, who got them from *her* mother, and so on.

In the mid-1980s geneticist Allan Wilson and associates at the University of California at Berkeley began a study of DNA from human mitochondria. Comparing DNA samples from people all over the world and considering the rate of mutations in human DNA, they calculated that all the humans alive today are the descendants of a single woman who lived in Africa about 200,000 years ago! Wilson called her "the mother of us all"; reporters soon nicknamed her "Eve." Not all scientists accept this finding, but if it is correct, it supports the idea that *Homo sapiens* first appeared in Africa and later spread to other parts of the world.

Our own species, *Homo sapiens* ("wise man"), evolved in Africa about 400,000 years ago and soon spread to Europe and Asia. By about 200,000 years ago, the now-famous Neanderthal Man evolved. The **Neanderthals** (commonly called cave men) were named for the Neander Valley in Germany, where the first human fossil of this type was discovered. (*Thal* means "valley" in German.)

Neanderthals were probably not our direct ancestors. They were once considered a subspecies of *Homo sapiens*. Now, however, some scientists regard Neanderthals as a separate species, naming them *Homo neanderthalensis*. Recently, researchers from the University of Munich and Penn State University removed DNA from the upper-arm bone of a Neanderthal fossil to compare it with that of modern humans. The scientists found significant differences—about twenty-seven mutations. These findings suggest that humans and Neanderthals split from a common ancestor about 600,000 years ago.

Neanderthals were short, stocky, muscular people who had protruding faces, noses, and foreheads, but lacked a defined chin. They had a large brain capacity, though, equaling or exceeding that of modern humans—1,200 to 1,750 cubic centimeters (73 to 107 cubic inches). Despite their primitive appearance, they were highly intelligent and had a complex culture. They made a variety of tools including scrapers, borers, hand axes, and spearheads. Neanderthals also took care of those who were sick and injured, as indicated by fossil skeletons with healed wounds. Fossils also indicate that Neanderthals buried their dead with weapons, food, and flowers, suggesting that they believed in an afterlife.

The first modern *Homo sapiens* appeared about 40,000 years ago. Fossils dated from that time indicate that they looked much like today's humans. Scientists classify modern humans as *Homo sapiens sapiens* (or *H. sapiens*). The Neanderthals died out about 34,000 years ago when they had to compete for food sources with the more modern humans, the **Cro-Magnons**. The Cro-Magnons had smaller faces and lacked the projecting features that the Neanderthals had. Their bodies were also more slender, their teeth were smaller, and their culture was much more complex. The Cro-Magnons had a brain capacity that was the same as today's humans (about 1,400 cubic centimeters, or 85 cubic inches, on the average).

Their tools, made of bone, ivory, and wood, were complicated and were used for a variety of purposes. Some scientists believe that the Cro-Magnons' use of these tools resulted in the extinction of the large mammals, such as the giant sloth, mammoths, saber-tooth tigers, and giant oxen. However, the Cro-Magnons are best known for their beautiful paintings on cave walls in Spain and France, and the many sculptures of small figurines. Their complex tools, along with their artistic expression, indicate that the Cro-Magnons may have been capable of language abilities, which allowed information to be passed on through generations.

Cro-Magnons did this painting of horses on a wall in Lascaux cave in France about 17,000 years ago.

✦ CULTURAL EVOLUTION ✦

About 20,000 to 15,000 years ago, humans were widespread throughout most regions of the world. They followed herds of mammoths, woolly rhinoceroses, reindeer, and other animals into the arctic regions of Eurasia and traveled across the Bering land bridge into the Americas. They also built boats and ventured into uncharted waters to New Guinea and Australia.

About 10,000 years ago in the Middle East, some people started to plant seeds to produce food crops. They also started to tame and domesticate wild animals for their milk, meat, and labor. Agriculture led to a more settled way of life, and some of the first towns and cities were built in places with good water and soil. Farmers traded surplus food for tools, baskets, and pots made by craftspeople.

Generation after generation, human cultures became increasingly complex as people acquired more skills and knowledge. This **cultural evolution** has allowed humans to gain some control over their environment, providing for more dependable food supplies and defense against predators and diseases. Thus we have reduced the effects of natural selection both on ourselves and on our domesticated animals. Humans are the only creatures that can control most aspects of their lives—and the lives of all other species.

SEVEN

EVOLUTION AND THE FUTURE

In his book *The Origin of Species*, Darwin wrote: "It may metaphorically be said that natural selection is daily and hourly scrutinizing, throughout the world, the slightest variations; rejecting those that are bad, preserving and adding up all that are good; silently and insensibly working, *whenever and wherever opportunity offers.*... We see nothing of these slow changes in progress, until the hand of time has marked the lapse of ages."

Today, when we hear the word *evolution*, we tend to think about fossils and the prehistoric people and animals that lived on earth millions of years ago. Like Darwin, we imagine a process so slow and gradual that we cannot witness it in a single lifetime—it can be seen only over long periods of time in geological history. What Darwin did not realize, however, was that natural selection was more powerful than he could have dreamed. Evolution is neither rare nor slow. Evolution occurs in our lives every single day, and we can watch it happen.

During the 1970s, for instance, researchers Peter and Rosemary Grant of Princeton University decided to travel to the Galápagos Islands, where Darwin observed the finches whose variations helped to shape his theory of evolution. The Grants and their associates camped out on a tiny desert island in an extinct volcano, called Daphne Major. They studied the various native species, especially "Darwin's finches." In 1977 the Grants witnessed a terrible drought on the island. Many animals died as a result. Flocks of *Geospiza fortis*, the most common finch on the island, numbered over 1,000 in January and were reduced to less than 200 in December. The Grants watched the birds evolve. The next generation of birds had beaks that were not only bigger but narrower and deeper. They were now sharp instruments that could open tough seeds. Darwin had never seen evolution work this quickly.

In 1983 torrential rains flooded the island. Daphne changed from a desert into a jungle practically overnight. While many finches died, others were productive. This time the next generation of *Geospiza fortis* had beaks that were much smaller, which allowed them to adapt to the tiny seeds that were overflowing on the new grassy island. The Grants continued to witness these birds evolve and recorded their progress.

The Grants' study was actually an expansion of Darwin's. They and their team proved that evolution is not something that occurred only in the past. Evolution continues to exist in the present, and it will be there in our future.

✦ OUR FUTURE EVOLUTION ✦

Can people control their own evolution? Will future generations be able to modify their children's traits so that, for example, they can breathe underwater without scuba gear, or make food by photosynthesis while sunbathing? Will some future generations evolve into people who can live comfortably in colonies on the moon or Mars?

What if we could create a population without any physical and mental defects? Scientists believe that more people today are carrying defective genes, a situation most likely due to exposure to radiation, chemicals, and other environmental hazards. Advanced technology in medicine, however, has made it possible for people with inherited diseases to live longer lives—and pass on their "bad genes" to their offspring.

A generation ago, scientists (and science-fiction writers) were warning that genetic defects would continue to accumulate until our world was filled with people totally dependent on high-tech medicine for survival. Recently, however, we have been learning more about the inner workings of our bodies. Techniques for **gene therapy** are being developed to correct genetic defects and cure diseases. "Birth technology" is a fast-growing field. Researchers can fertilize a single human egg with a single sperm in a test tube or laboratory culture dish and can screen embryos for a variety of defects.

It seems likely that we will ultimately be able to select desirable traits for our children, even such complex traits as intelligence or sports ability. But who will

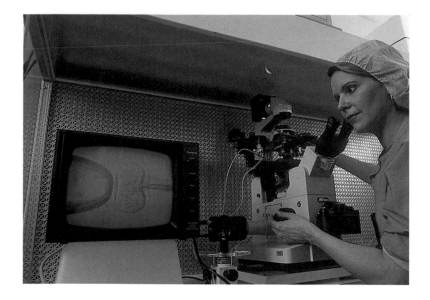

The screen shows an enlarged image of a human egg being prepared for in vitro fertilization. The scientist is scratching the egg, which will make it easier for the sperm to penetrate the egg.

decide what is "desirable," and will the decisions be wise ones? Do we run the risk of overspecializing, of breeding out traits that do not seem important now but might be needed if our environment should change suddenly? Or will we gain such fine control over our environment that we can keep it suitable for our needs? And then will *Homo sapiens* die of boredom?

✦ THE NEVER-ENDING STRUGGLE FOR SURVIVAL ✦

So far, at least, it seems that our environment will continue to hold enough surprises to keep life challenging. The forces that nature can pack into a hurricane or a volcanic eruption top anything that humans can produce or control. The living world provides continuing challenges as well. Human activities have been interfering with some of the natural processes of evolution on our planet. People have been cutting down forests and polluting the air and water. As a result, we are in the midst of another great wave of extinctions. Biologists warn that the earth's biodiversity is decreasing rapidly. In rain forests and other vanishing wild areas, many species are becoming extinct before we even discover them. Who knows what valuable knowledge we could have gained from them? New insights into life's history, new foods and drugs—many new opportunities may already be lost.

Meanwhile, evolution is also transforming earth's microworld in ways that may challenge our survival. The discovery of antibiotics and vaccines, for exam-

This rain forest in Brazil was burned with little regard for the loss of species. The land was cleared for cattle ranching.

ple, seemed for a while to spell the end for infectious diseases. In the industrially developed nations, sickness and death from old killers such as tuberculosis and diphtheria were becoming rare. Now, however, some of the old diseases are making a comeback, and public-health experts are worried that new "emerging diseases" can break out of places like rural villages in Africa and sweep through the world. AIDS was totally unknown before the 1980s, and now this viral disease has become an exploding threat to world health. Scary new plagues such as Ebola could be making headlines tomorrow.

In 1997 a sheep named Dolly made the headlines. She was a clone, a sort of identical twin produced by laboratory manipulations that inserted DNA from a cell in her mother's mammary gland into a sheep egg that was then transplanted into the uterus of an unrelated "surrogate mother" sheep. Since then, animals of other species have been cloned successfully, and in a highly controversial idea, researchers are speculating that we may be able to clone humans someday. Meanwhile, it has been suggested that we could clone animals of extinct species if we can find DNA samples in good enough condition.

So far, the idea of cloning dinosaurs (perhaps from DNA in fossilized dinosaur eggs) is still just a fantasy for science-fiction stories, but a group of researchers is actually trying to do something about bringing back woolly mammoths. A team of researchers from Japan, Russia, and Britain have been searching the ice fields of Siberia, hoping to find frozen woolly mammoths. If researchers can find some, they hope to use mammoth sperm to fertilize elephant ova, then breed back the half-elephant offspring to produce animals genetically similar to the mammoths that roamed the earth 10,000 years ago.

Viruses, bacteria, and other parasites are facing their own struggles for survival, and the forces of natural selection are operating on them, too. One advantage they have is a very short life cycle. A virus may produce a new generation of offspring in just hours or even minutes. Typically it has large numbers of offspring and can mutate rapidly enough to develop resistance to many of the new drugs we are devising to fight diseases. Viruses, bacteria, and other disease-causing microbes are evolving right now. One of the big challenges for tomorrow's medicine will be to find ways to shape their evolution, so that they will become less harmful rather than more deadly.

GLOSSARY

adaptation—a change in an organism making it more fit for particular environmental conditions.

aerobe—an organism that utilizes oxygen in its life processes.

anaerobe—an organism that lives in the absence of oxygen.

anthropoids—a group of higher primates including monkeys, apes, and humans.

Archeozoic Era—the time during which the earth was forming.

arthropods—invertebrates with jointed legs.

artificial selection—selective breeding of plants and animals by humans to produce offspring with specific desirable traits.

autotroph—an organism that produces its own food.

binocular vision—vision in which both eyes work together, providing three-dimensional depth perception.

biochemistry—the science of the chemical compounds found in living organisms and their reactions.

Cenozoic Era—the fifth era in the evolution of the earth, during which placental mammals became dominant; includes the present time.

chemical evolution—the formation of early life forms by spontaneous joining of organic (carbon-containing) chemicals.

chromosomes—structures containing genes, found within the nucleus of a cell.

clone—an offspring produced by transfer of DNA (the chemicals of heredity) from a body cell of the parent, producing an "identical twin." The term is also used for a group of cells or organisms, all produced from a single cell and sharing the same heredity.

convergent evolution—the development of similar structures or adaptations by species that are not closely related.

creationism—the theory that each species of living organism on earth was created separately, in the same form in which it exists today.

Cro-Magnons—the first modern humans.

cultural evolution—the development of increasingly complex skills and knowledge, shared among members of human populations and transmitted from one generation to the next.

darwinism—the theory of evolution developed and popularized by Charles Darwin, stating that new species developed by a process of natural selection.

dinosaurs—various species of reptiles that lived during the Mesozoic Era.

divergent evolution—the development of different species from a common ancestor.

dominant trait—a hereditary characteristic that always appears in the offspring even if inherited from only one parent.

embryo—an early stage that organisms go through during their development before birth.

epoch—a subdivision of a geological period.

era—a geological time period marked by a significant geological or biological event in the evolution of life.

evolution—the development of new types of living organisms by the accumulation of genetic changes over time.

extinction—the disappearance of all living members of a species.

fermentation—a breakdown of energy-rich organic molecules that does not require oxygen.

fossil—the preserved remains or traces of living organisms of the past.

gene therapy—the manipulation and transfer of genes to correct hereditary defects.

genes—chemical units that determine hereditary traits passed on from one generation of cells or organisms to the next.

half-life—the time in which half of a portion of a radioisotope decays (is changed to another isotope).

heterotroph—an organism that gets food materials by feeding on other organisms.

hominids—the first humanlike primates (Australopithecines).

hominoids—the great apes, including gibbons, orangutans, gorillas, and chimpanzees.

Homo—the genus including early humans and the present-day human species, *Homo sapiens.*

homologous structures—organs or body parts of different species with a similar internal structure, suggesting a common origin.

hybrid—an offspring of cross-breeding between two species or groups.

invertebrates—animals without backbones.

isolation—the separation of two breeding populations by a physical barrier, a different habitat or lifestyle, or genetic mutations that prevent interbreeding.

isotopes—forms of an element that differ in atomic weight and other properties; those that emit radiations and decay (gradually change to other isotopes) are called **radioisotopes**.

mammals—vertebrates with fur that produce milk to feed their young.

marsupials—early mammals whose young are born in a very immature stage and complete their development in a pouch on the mother's abdomen (the **marsupium**). Most of the surviving marsupial species are native to Australia.

Mesozoic Era—the fourth era in the evolution of the earth, during which reptiles dominated the land, sea, and air.

mitochondria—structures inside the cell that generate energy for life processes and have their own set of genes, inherited separately from the chromosomes.

monotremes—early mammals that laid eggs but had milk-producing mammary glands to feed their young; the only surviving monotremes live in Australia.

mutation—a change in a gene or genes that can be passed on to the next generation.

natural selection—a process of evolution in which living organisms compete for survival, and those best suited for the environmental conditions survive and produce offspring; also called **survival of the fittest**.

Neanderthals—a type of early humans considered by some scientists as a separate species.

Paleozoic Era—the third era in the evolution of the earth, which began with the appearance of the first aerobes and included the development of the first animals.

period—a subdivision of a geological era.

photosynthesis—a process of food production from simple chemicals, utilizing sunlight energy.

placental mammals—mammals that provide their developing offspring with nourishment through an organ called the **placenta** inside the mother's body.

Precambrian Time—the Archeozoic and Proterozoic Eras.

primates—an order of mammals including tree shrews, tarsiers, lemurs, monkeys, apes, and humans.

prosimians—a group of lower primates including tarsiers and lemurs.

Proterozoic Era—the second era in the evolution of the earth, which began with the appearance of the first living organisms.

recessive trait—a hereditary characteristic that appears in the offspring only if it has been inherited from both parents.

sedimentary rocks—rocks formed in layers, which may preserve fossils and permit their relative placement in past time.

speciation—the development of a new species.

species—a particular group or population of organisms sharing genetic characteristics and (usually) unable to breed with organisms of other groups.

stratigraphy—the study of the earth's strata (rock layers).

vertebrates—animals with an internal skeleton, including a backbone.

FOR FURTHER INFORMATION

BOOKS

Anderson, Margaret J., *Charles Darwin: Naturalist.* Springfield, NJ: Enslow, 1994.

Ankerberg, John and John Weldon, *The Facts on Creation vs. Evolution.* New York: Harvest House, 1993.

Fortey, Richard, *Fossils: The Key to the Past.* Cambridge, MA: Harvard University Press, 1994.

Gamblin, Linda, *Evolution (Eyewitness Science).* New York: Dorling-Kindersley, 1993.

Gould, Stephen Jay, *The Book of Life: An Illustrated History of the Evolution of Life on Earth.* New York: W. W. Norton, 1993.

Hoagland, Mahlon and Bert Dodson, *The Way Life Works.* New York: Times Books, 1995.

Horner, John R. and Edwin Dobb, *Dinosaur Lives: Unearthing an Evolutionary Saga.* New York, HarperCollins, 1997.

Kitcher, Philip, *Abusing Science: The Case Against Creationism.* Cambridge, MA: MIT Press, 1984.

Lewin, Roger, *Bones of Contention: Controversies in the Search for Human Origins.* Chicago: University of Chicago Press, 1997.

Lindsay, William, *Prehistoric Life.* New York: Knopf, 1994.

Ruiz, Andres Llamas, *Evolution.* New York: Sterling Publications, 1997.

Stein, Sara Bonnett, *The Evolution Book.* New York: Workman, 1986.

Stringer, Christopher and Robin McKie, *African Exodus: The Origins of Modern Humanity.* New York: Henry Holt, 1997.

Twist, Clint, *Charles Darwin: On the Trail of Evolution.* Chatham, NJ: Raintree/ Steck-Vaughn, 1994.

Ventura, Piero, *Darwin: Nature Reinterpreted.* Boston: Houghton Mifflin, 1995

Weiner, Jonathan, *The Beak of the Finch: A Story of Evolution in Our Time.* New York: Knopf, 1994.

Whitfield, Philip, *From So Simple a Beginning: The Book of Evolution.* New York: Macmillan, 1995.

Young, David, *The Discovery of Evolution.* New York: Cambridge University Press, 1993.

INTERNET RESOURCES

http://bioinfo.med.utoronto.ca/~lamoran/Evolution_home.shtml "Evolution Homepage" [links to information on evolution, the fossil record, classification, evolution and religion, and references]

http://denr1.igis.uiuc.edu:/isgsroot/dinos/dinos_home.html Russell J. Jacobson, "Dino Russ's Lair" [dinosaur art, information, exhibits, news, organizations, sites, and lots of links]

http://field.netscape.com/~jfb/dino_hotlinks.html "Dinosaur Hotlinks" [links to dinosaur art and information pages]

http://golgi.harvard.edu/biopages/evolution.html "The World Wide Web Virtual Library: Evolution (Biosciences)" [links to journals, societies, evolution information, museums, etc.]

http://web.syr.edu/~dbgoldma/pictures.html David Goldman, "Dinosaur Illustrations" [click on a dinosaur's name to see a picture of it]

http://weber.u.washington.edu/~jahayes/evolution/index.html "Welcome to the Sci.Bio.Evolution home page!" [links to evolution resources, artificial life, fossils, media resources, and some "fringe ideas" such as the Aquatic Ape Theory page]

http://www.cen.uiuc.edu/~priestle/aa/ Matthew Priestley, "Take the Lucy Test" [compare photos of fossil bones and decide for yourself how they are related]

http://www.dinosauria.com/jdp/jdp.htm "Jeff's Journal of Dinosaur Paleontology" [links to many dinosaur sites with a brief description of each]

http://www.geocities.com/CapeCanaveral/1179/evolink.html "Links to Evolution Pages" [links to some evolution sites, including some "bad pages," with a brief description of each]

http://www.geocities.com/CapeCanaveral/1179/evolve.html "Emily and August's Evolution Pages" [links and information about evolution, misunderstandings of evolution, and recent developments]

http://www.kirtland.cc.mi.us/honors/adam/adamevol.htm "Adam's Evolution Page" [evolution and information links prepared by a ninth-grade biology student]

http://www.primate.wisc.edu/pin/evolution.html "Primate Evolution" [links to information on human and primate evolution]

http://www.religioustolerance.org/ev_evol.htm "What Are Evolution and Creation Science" [detailed comparison of evolutionary theory and creationism]

http://www.religioustolerance.org/evolutio.htm "Theory of Evolution vs. Creation Science" [discussion and links to the debate between evolution and creation science]

http://www-sci.lib.uci.edu/SEP/life.html#5 "Frank Potter's Science Gems - Life Science" [links to various life science sites, including a collection of evolution sites, with a description of each and grouped according to grade level of content]

http://www.spacelab.net/~catalj/ John Catalano, "The World of Richard Dawkins" [links to evolution news, sites, book reviews, and information on researcher Richard Dawkins]

http://www.stg.brown.edu/projects/hypertext/landow/victorian/darwin/darwinov.html "Darwin and Evolution Overview" [a section of the Victorian Site devoted to Charles Darwin, his work, and his theory of evolution]

http://www.talkorigins.org/origins/faqs-evolution.html "The Talk Origins Archive: Biology and Evolutionary Theory" [many long evolution FAQs ("Frequently Asked Questions") and essays on evolutionary theory, the work of Charles Darwin (including the full text of *The Origin of Species*), evidence for evolution, fossils, etc.]

http://www.trollart.com/EVOLUTION.html "Ray Troll's Finart: Evolution" [humorous original art and commentary with interactive animations of "Evolvovision"]

http://www.ucmp.berkeley.edu/fosrec/fosrec.html "Learning from the Fossil Record" [links to fossil resources and classroom activities]

http://www.ucmp.berkeley.edu/history/evolution.html "Enter Evolution: Theory and History" [essays on Charles Darwin and other scientists associated with evolution]

http://www.west.net/~ljfries/evo.htm Larry Jon Friesen, "Evolution and Adaptation" [links to evolution illustrations and information]

http://www.yahoo.com/Science/Biology/Evolution/index.html "Yahoo!—Science:Biology:Evolution" [links to evolution sites compiled by the search engine Yahoo!]

http://www.zoomschool.com/subjects/dinosaurs/dinofossils/Fossilfind.html "Finding Dinosaur Fossils—Enchanted Learning Software" [information about where and how fossils are found]

INDEX